EMMANUEL JOSEPH

From Asgard to Anatomy, The Mythological Foundations of Medicine and Architecture

Copyright © 2025 by Emmanuel Joseph

All rights reserved. No part of this publication may be reproduced, stored or transmitted in any form or by any means, electronic, mechanical, photocopying, recording, scanning, or otherwise without written permission from the publisher. It is illegal to copy this book, post it to a website, or distribute it by any other means without permission.

First edition

This book was professionally typeset on Reedsy. Find out more at reedsy.com

Contents

1 Chapter 1: The Mythological Backdrop — 1
2 Chapter 2: The Healers of Olympus — 3
3 Chapter 3: Norse Anatomy and the Vital Spirit — 5
4 Chapter 4: The Architectural Marvels of Egypt — 7
5 Chapter 5: Roman Temples and Healing Sanctuaries — 9
6 Chapter 6: The Symbolism of Sacred Geometry — 11
7 Chapter 7: The Alchemical Body — 13
8 Chapter 8: The Healing Waters of the Celts — 15
9 Chapter 7: The Alchemical Body — 17
10 Chapter 8: The Healing Waters of the Celts — 19
11 Chapter 9: The Cosmic Architecture of the Mayans — 21
12 Chapter 10: The Medicine Wheel of the Native Americans — 23
13 Chapter 11: The Renaissance Revival of Myth — 25
14 Chapter 12: The Legacy of Myth in Modern Medicine and... — 27
15 Chapter 13: The Divine Proportion and the Human Body — 29
16 Chapter 14: The Symbolism of Light in Sacred Spaces — 31
17 Chapter 15: Mythological Inspirations in Contemporary... — 33

1

Chapter 1: The Mythological Backdrop

In the ancient world, mythology was more than just a collection of stories; it was a framework for understanding the cosmos, humanity, and the natural world. From the lofty peaks of Olympus to the celestial halls of Asgard, these myths provided a blueprint for the societies that worshipped them. They defined the gods' influence on everyday life and offered explanations for the mysteries of nature, from the cycle of seasons to the origins of life itself. This chapter explores how these mythologies formed the bedrock upon which early civilizations built their knowledge and practices, including those in medicine and architecture.

Mythological tales often depicted gods and heroes engaging in acts that had profound implications for human understanding and societal norms. The adventures of deities such as Zeus, Thor, and Ra were not just entertaining stories but carried symbolic meanings that informed cultural values and practices. For instance, the ancient Egyptians' belief in the afterlife influenced their burial practices and the construction of monumental tombs. Similarly, the Norse mythology of Ragnarok, the end of the world, shaped their view of life, death, and the cyclical nature of existence.

These mythologies also served as a means of preserving and transmitting knowledge across generations. In an era before written records were widespread, oral traditions played a crucial role in maintaining cultural continuity. Storytellers, priests, and shamans were the custodians of this knowledge, passing down intricate tales that intertwined with practical wisdom. This blend of myth and reality created a rich tapestry that guided early societies in their quest to understand the world and their place within it.

As civilizations grew and developed, their mythological foundations evolved, incorporating new ideas and adapting to changing circumstances. The introduction of writing allowed for the codification of myths, ensuring their survival and facilitating their spread across different cultures. This process of adaptation and reinterpretation continued to influence the development of medical and architectural knowledge, as ancient myths provided a source of inspiration and a framework for innovation.

2

Chapter 2: The Healers of Olympus

Greek mythology is rich with tales of gods and mortals possessing extraordinary healing abilities. Asclepius, the god of medicine, wielded the power to cure diseases and even bring the dead back to life. Temples dedicated to Asclepius, known as Asclepieia, became centers for medical treatment and learning. Here, priests interpreted dreams and prescribed treatments, blending divine inspiration with empirical practices. This chapter delves into how these mythological foundations laid the groundwork for early medical knowledge and institutions, influencing the development of hospitals and medical schools.

The legend of Asclepius is particularly significant in the context of ancient Greek medicine. According to myth, Asclepius was the son of Apollo and a mortal woman, Coronis. He was taught the art of healing by the centaur Chiron and became so skilled that he could even resurrect the dead. This ability eventually led to his downfall, as Zeus, fearing the disruption of the natural order, struck him down with a thunderbolt. Despite his tragic end, Asclepius's legacy lived on through the temples built in his honor, which served as early hospitals where patients sought cures for their ailments.

These temples, known as Asclepieia, were not just places of worship but also centers for medical knowledge and practice. Priests, known as Asclepiads, acted as both religious and medical practitioners, interpreting the will of the gods and providing treatments based on a combination of divine inspiration and empirical observation. Patients would undergo rituals such as dream incubation, where they slept in the temple and received healing insights through their dreams. These practices, rooted in mythological beliefs, contributed to the development of early medical traditions and the establishment of healthcare institutions.

The influence of Asclepius extended beyond the boundaries of Greece, as his cult spread throughout the Mediterranean and into Roman territories. The Romans adopted and adapted Greek medical practices, incorporating them into their own healthcare system. The symbol of the rod of Asclepius, a staff entwined with a serpent, became an enduring emblem of medicine and healing, reflecting the deep-rooted connection between mythology and medical practice. This enduring legacy highlights the profound impact of mythological foundations on the evolution of medical knowledge and institutions.

3

Chapter 3: Norse Anatomy and the Vital Spirit

In Norse mythology, the human body was seen as a microcosm of the universe, influenced by the divine and natural forces that shaped the world. The gods themselves were subject to physical ailments and sought remedies to maintain their health and vitality. The Norse believed in a vital spirit, or "hamingja," that sustained life and health. This chapter examines the intersection of Norse mythological beliefs and their understanding of anatomy, highlighting how these ideas permeated their medical practices and influenced the treatment of injuries and illnesses.

The Norse sagas and eddas are replete with references to the physical and spiritual health of both gods and mortals. For instance, the god Baldr was revered for his beauty and invulnerability, but even he fell victim to a fatal wound, underscoring the fragility of life. The myth of Baldr's death and subsequent attempts to resurrect him reflect the Norse fascination with healing and the afterlife. These stories informed their medical practices, where healers would invoke the gods and use natural remedies, such as herbs and rituals, to treat ailments.

The concept of "hamingja" was central to Norse medical beliefs. This vital spirit was thought to be a source of strength, luck, and health, and its presence or absence could determine an individual's well-being. The Norse believed that maintaining a balance between the body, mind, and spirit was essential for good health. This holistic approach to medicine influenced their treatment methods, which often involved a combination of physical remedies, spiritual invocations, and communal support.

Architecturally, the Norse built structures that reflected their cosmological beliefs and their understanding of the human body's connection to the universe. Longhouses, temples, and burial mounds were constructed with symbolic elements that represented the gods and the natural world. These buildings served as both functional spaces and sacred sites, where rituals were performed to ensure the health and prosperity of the community. The integration of mythological beliefs into their architecture underscores the profound influence of these narratives on their everyday lives.

4

Chapter 4: The Architectural Marvels of Egypt

Ancient Egyptian mythology played a crucial role in the design and construction of their monumental architecture. The pyramids, temples, and tombs were not merely structures but representations of cosmic order and divine power. The alignment of these buildings with celestial bodies and their intricate carvings depicting mythological scenes served both religious and practical purposes. In this chapter, we explore how Egyptian myths inspired their architectural feats, leading to innovations in construction techniques and urban planning that would influence subsequent civilizations.

The Egyptians believed that the pharaohs were divine beings, descendants of the gods who played a vital role in maintaining ma'at, or cosmic order. This belief was reflected in the grandiosity and precision of their architectural projects. The pyramids, for example, were designed as eternal resting places for the pharaohs, constructed with mathematical precision to align with the stars and ensure the pharaohs' journey to the afterlife. These structures symbolized the connection between the earthly and the divine, embodying the Egyptians' mythological worldview.

Temples were another significant aspect of Egyptian architecture, serving as houses for the gods and centers for religious rituals. The Temple of

Karnak, dedicated to the god Amun, is one of the most impressive examples of Egyptian temple architecture. Its massive columns, intricate carvings, and sacred lake were designed to reflect the power and majesty of the gods. The temple complex served as a spiritual and administrative center, where priests performed rituals, offerings were made, and political decisions were influenced by divine guidance.

The mythology of the afterlife profoundly influenced Egyptian burial practices and the construction of tombs. The belief in an eternal life beyond death led to the development of elaborate burial chambers, filled with treasures, amulets, and inscriptions to protect and guide the deceased in the afterlife. The tombs of the Valley of the Kings, with their hidden entrances and richly decorated interiors, exemplify the Egyptians' devotion to ensuring a safe passage to the afterlife. These architectural innovations were not only a testament to their engineering skills but also a reflection of their deep-seated mythological beliefs.

5

Chapter 5: Roman Temples and Healing Sanctuaries

The Romans inherited and adapted much of their mythology and architectural knowledge from the Greeks. They built magnificent temples dedicated to their gods, who were often borrowed from Greek mythology and given new names and attributes. Healing sanctuaries, such as the Temple of Aesculapius on Tiber Island, combined religious devotion with medical treatment. This chapter investigates the Roman approach to architecture and medicine, highlighting how their mythological beliefs shaped the design and function of their buildings and public spaces.

Roman mythology, like its Greek counterpart, was rich with deities and heroes who played a crucial role in shaping the cultural and religious landscape. The Romans believed that the gods influenced every aspect of their lives, from personal health to the success of the empire. This belief was reflected in the construction of temples and public buildings, which served as centers for worship, political gatherings, and community activities. The grandeur and architectural innovation of these structures demonstrated the Romans' reverence for their gods and their desire to gain divine favor.

One of the most notable examples of Roman architectural ingenuity influenced by mythology is the Pantheon. Originally built as a temple to all the gods, the Pantheon boasts a massive domed roof with a central oculus, symbolizing the heavens. The harmonious proportions and use of concrete as a building material were groundbreaking for the time and influenced architectural design for centuries to come. The Pantheon's design reflects the Romans' desire to create a structure that embodied the order and unity of the cosmos.

The Temple of Aesculapius on Tiber Island is another significant example of the intersection of mythology and medical practice in Roman architecture. Dedicated to Aesculapius, the god of healing, this temple served as a sanctuary for those seeking medical treatment. Patients would make offerings and participate in rituals to invoke the god's healing powers. The temple complex included facilities for bathing, sleeping, and medical treatments, blending religious devotion with practical healthcare. This integration of mythological beliefs into medical practice highlights the Romans' holistic approach to health and wellness.

The influence of Roman mythology on architecture extended to the design of public spaces such as forums, baths, and amphitheaters. These spaces were not only functional but also imbued with symbolic meaning, reflecting the Romans' values and their reverence for the gods. The Forum, for example, was the political and social heart of the city, where temples, basilicas, and public buildings coexisted, creating a space that symbolized the unity and strength of the Roman state. This seamless integration of mythology into architectural design underscores the enduring legacy of Roman innovation and its impact on subsequent civilizations.

6

Chapter 6: The Symbolism of Sacred Geometry

Sacred geometry is a concept found in many ancient cultures, where geometric shapes and proportions were believed to have divine significance. From the intricate mandalas of Hinduism and Buddhism to the geometric patterns in Islamic architecture, these shapes were thought to reflect the underlying order of the universe. This chapter explores the mythological foundations of sacred geometry and its application in both medicine and architecture, demonstrating how these ancient principles continue to influence modern design and healing practices.

The concept of sacred geometry is rooted in the belief that certain shapes and proportions are fundamental to the structure of the cosmos and hold spiritual power. This idea can be traced back to the ancient Egyptians, who used geometric principles in the design of their pyramids and temples. The Great Pyramid of Giza, for example, is built with precise mathematical proportions that align with the cardinal points and celestial bodies. This alignment was believed to facilitate the pharaoh's journey to the afterlife, reflecting the Egyptians' understanding of the cosmos and their place within it.

In Hinduism and Buddhism, sacred geometry is embodied in the design of mandalas, which are intricate geometric patterns used for meditation and spiritual practice. These patterns represent the universe and the interconnectedness of all life, serving as a visual aid for spiritual growth and enlightenment. The use of mandalas in temples and religious art highlights the importance of geometry in conveying spiritual truths and connecting the material world with the divine.

Islamic architecture also makes extensive use of sacred geometry, with intricate patterns and designs that adorn mosques, palaces, and public buildings. These geometric patterns, known as arabesques, are characterized by their complex symmetry and repetition, symbolizing the infinite nature of Allah. The use of geometry in Islamic art and architecture reflects the belief in a divine order that governs the universe, and the desire to create spaces that inspire spiritual reflection and connection with the divine.

The principles of sacred geometry have also influenced the field of medicine, particularly in the design of healing spaces. The ancient Greeks, for example, believed that the harmony and proportion of the human body were reflections of a divine order. This idea is embodied in the concept of the "golden ratio," a mathematical proportion that is found in the natural world and has been used in art, architecture, and medicine for centuries. The application of sacred geometry in the design of hospitals, healing gardens, and therapeutic spaces reflects the enduring belief in the power of geometric harmony to promote health and well-being.

7

Chapter 7: The Alchemical Body

Alchemy, with its roots in ancient Egyptian, Greek, and Arabic traditions, sought to transform base materials into noble ones and unlock the secrets of life and immortality. Alchemists viewed the human body as a vessel for divine energy, capable of being purified and perfected. This chapter examines the mythological underpinnings of alchemy and its impact on early medical theories and practices, tracing the evolution of alchemical thought and its lasting influence on both medicine and architecture.

The practice of alchemy was deeply intertwined with mythology and spiritual beliefs. In ancient Egypt, the god Thoth was revered as the patron of alchemy, knowledge, and writing. Egyptian alchemists sought to harness the divine wisdom of Thoth to transform materials and achieve spiritual enlightenment. The Greek alchemist Zosimos of Panopolis further developed these ideas, blending Egyptian and Greek mythological concepts. He believed that alchemy was not only a physical process but also a spiritual journey, involving the purification of the soul and the attainment of divine knowledge.

Arabic alchemy, which flourished during the Islamic Golden Age, was influenced by the works of Greek and Egyptian alchemists and enriched by Islamic philosophy and science. The legendary figure of Hermes Trismegistus, a fusion of the Greek god Hermes and the Egyptian god Thoth, became a central figure in Islamic alchemical tradition. Alchemical texts attributed to

Hermes, known as Hermetic writings, emphasized the interconnectedness of the material and spiritual worlds, reflecting the belief that the human body could be transformed and perfected through alchemical practices.

The influence of alchemy extended beyond medicine to architecture, as alchemists believed that the principles of transformation and harmony could be applied to the design of buildings and cities. Alchemical symbols and motifs were incorporated into architectural designs, creating spaces that embodied the alchemical quest for balance and unity. The use of sacred geometry in alchemical architecture reflected the belief that geometric shapes and proportions held the key to unlocking the secrets of the cosmos and achieving spiritual transformation. This integration of alchemical thought into both medicine and architecture highlights the enduring impact of these mythological foundations.

8

Chapter 8: The Healing Waters of the Celts

Celtic mythology is replete with references to sacred wells and healing springs, believed to be imbued with the power of the gods and spirits. These natural water sources were often associated with specific deities and were sites of pilgrimage and ritual healing. In this chapter, we explore the role of water in Celtic medicine and architecture, examining how these mythological beliefs shaped the construction of wells, baths, and other water-related structures that served both practical and spiritual purposes.

The Celts believed that certain natural springs and wells were blessed with divine healing properties, often attributed to deities such as Brigid, the goddess of healing, poetry, and smithcraft. Pilgrims would visit these sacred sites to seek cures for their ailments, perform rituals, and offer votive gifts. The waters of these springs were believed to possess magical properties that could cleanse the body and soul, reflecting the Celts' deep connection to the natural world and their belief in the interconnectedness of physical and spiritual health.

Architectural evidence of these beliefs can be seen in the construction of wells and baths throughout Celtic lands. These structures were often elaborately designed, with stone carvings and inscriptions dedicated to the gods and spirits associated with the water. The architecture of these healing sites reflects the Celts' reverence for nature and their desire to create spaces that facilitated both physical healing and spiritual renewal. The integration of mythological motifs and symbols into the design of these structures underscores the importance of water in Celtic culture and medicine.

In addition to healing wells and springs, the Celts also built communal baths, which served as both social and therapeutic spaces. These baths were often located near sacred water sources and were designed to promote relaxation, cleansing, and healing. The architecture of these baths incorporated elements of both practicality and spirituality, with

9

Chapter 7: The Alchemical Body

Alchemy, with its roots in ancient Egyptian, Greek, and Arabic traditions, sought to transform base materials into noble ones and unlock the secrets of life and immortality. Alchemists viewed the human body as a vessel for divine energy, capable of being purified and perfected. This chapter examines the mythological underpinnings of alchemy and its impact on early medical theories and practices, tracing the evolution of alchemical thought and its lasting influence on both medicine and architecture.

The origins of alchemy can be traced back to ancient Egypt, where practitioners sought to transmute base metals into gold and achieve immortality. These early alchemists believed that the process of transformation mirrored the creation and renewal of life, a concept rooted in Egyptian mythology. The god Thoth, associated with wisdom and magic, was often invoked in alchemical practices. This blend of mythological beliefs and practical experimentation laid the groundwork for the development of alchemical traditions in later civilizations.

Greek alchemy built upon Egyptian foundations, incorporating philosophical and spiritual elements. The Greek alchemist Zosimos of Panopolis wrote extensively on the subject, describing alchemy as both a physical and spiritual journey. He believed that the purification of metals was analogous to the purification of the soul, a concept that resonated with the mythological themes of death and rebirth. Greek alchemy emphasized the connection between the microcosm (the human body) and the macrocosm (the universe), reflecting the belief in a divine order that governed both.

In the medieval Islamic world, alchemy reached new heights as scholars translated and expanded upon the works of their Greek and Egyptian predecessors. The renowned alchemist Jabir ibn Hayyan, known in the West as Geber, made significant contributions to the field, introducing new techniques and concepts. Islamic alchemists viewed their work as a way to understand the divine mysteries of creation and to achieve spiritual enlightenment. This integration of alchemical and religious beliefs influenced both medical practices and architectural designs, as alchemists sought to create harmonious spaces that reflected the divine order.

The legacy of alchemy can be seen in the development of modern chemistry and pharmacology, as well as in the design of healing spaces and architectural structures that embody the principles of transformation and harmony. The alchemical pursuit of perfection and balance continues to inspire contemporary thinkers and practitioners, demonstrating the enduring influence of mythological foundations on scientific and architectural innovation.

10

Chapter 8: The Healing Waters of the Celts

Celtic mythology is replete with references to sacred wells and healing springs, believed to be imbued with the power of the gods and spirits. These natural water sources were often associated with specific deities and were sites of pilgrimage and ritual healing. In this chapter, we explore the role of water in Celtic medicine and architecture, examining how these mythological beliefs shaped the construction of wells, baths, and other water-related structures that served both practical and spiritual purposes.

The Celts held a deep reverence for natural water sources, viewing them as gateways to the divine and sources of healing and renewal. Wells and springs dedicated to deities such as Brigid, the goddess of healing and poetry, were considered sacred and were often the site of rituals and offerings. Pilgrims would visit these sites to seek cures for ailments, offering tokens and prayers in exchange for the gods' favor. This practice reflects the Celtic belief in the interconnectedness of the physical and spiritual realms.

Architecturally, the Celts constructed elaborate wells and baths that incorporated both practical and symbolic elements. These structures were designed to harness the healing properties of water while also serving as places of worship and community gathering. The use of stone and other natural materials in their construction reflected the Celts' respect for the natural world and their desire to create harmonious spaces that resonated with their mythological beliefs.

The significance of water in Celtic mythology extended to their understanding of the human body and health. The Celts believed that water could cleanse not only the physical body but also the spirit, and they used it in various healing practices. Herbal remedies and poultices were often combined with water rituals to enhance their efficacy, reflecting the holistic approach to medicine that characterized Celtic healing traditions. This integration of mythological and practical knowledge highlights the Celts' sophisticated understanding of health and wellness.

The influence of Celtic water mythology can still be seen today in the continued reverence for natural springs and wells in many parts of the world. Modern spas and healing centers often draw on these ancient traditions, offering treatments that combine water therapy with spiritual practices. This enduring legacy underscores the profound impact of Celtic mythology on contemporary approaches to health and architecture, demonstrating the timeless relevance of these ancient beliefs.

11

Chapter 9: The Cosmic Architecture of the Mayans

The Mayan civilization, with its advanced knowledge of astronomy and mathematics, built cities and ceremonial centers that reflected their mythological understanding of the cosmos. The alignment of their buildings with celestial events and the incorporation of mythological motifs in their architecture were intended to harmonize the human and divine realms. This chapter delves into the mythological foundations of Mayan architecture, highlighting the ways in which their beliefs influenced the design and function of their built environment.

Mayan mythology was deeply intertwined with their understanding of the cosmos, and this connection was reflected in their architectural designs. The Mayans believed that the universe was governed by cycles of creation and destruction, and their buildings were constructed to align with celestial events such as solstices, equinoxes, and planetary movements. This alignment was believed to facilitate communication with the gods and ensure the prosperity and stability of their society.

The city of Chichen Itza is a prime example of Mayan cosmic architecture. The Temple of Kukulkan, also known as El Castillo, is a stepped pyramid that serves as a calendar and a symbol of the Mayan cosmology. During the equinoxes, the setting sun creates a serpent-like shadow on the pyramid's steps, symbolizing the descent of the god Kukulkan. This architectural marvel reflects the Mayans' advanced knowledge of astronomy and their belief in the interconnectedness of the natural and divine worlds.

Mythological motifs and symbols were also incorporated into the decoration and layout of Mayan buildings. Temples and palaces were adorned with carvings depicting gods, heroes, and mythological scenes, serving both religious and educational purposes. These intricate designs conveyed the Mayans' spiritual beliefs and cultural values, creating spaces that were both visually stunning and imbued with meaning. The integration of art and architecture in Mayan society highlights the importance of mythology in shaping their built environment.

The influence of Mayan cosmic architecture extends beyond their civilization, as their knowledge and practices were passed down through generations and adopted by other cultures. Today, the principles of Mayan architecture continue to inspire modern designers and architects, who seek to create buildings that reflect the harmony and balance of the natural world. This enduring legacy underscores the lasting impact of Mayan mythology on the field of architecture and our understanding of the cosmos.

12

Chapter 10: The Medicine Wheel of the Native Americans

The Medicine Wheel, a symbol used by various Native American tribes, represents the interconnectedness of all life and the cycles of nature. It is both a spiritual and practical tool, used for healing, teaching, and community gatherings. This chapter explores the mythological origins of the Medicine Wheel and its application in Native American medicine and architecture, demonstrating how these indigenous beliefs continue to shape their cultural practices and built environment.

The Medicine Wheel is a circular symbol divided into four quadrants, each representing different aspects of life, such as the four seasons, the four cardinal directions, and the stages of human life. It embodies the Native American belief in the cyclical nature of existence and the interconnectedness of all living beings. The center of the wheel represents balance and harmony, a concept that is central to Native American spirituality and healing practices.

In Native American medicine, the Medicine Wheel is used as a diagnostic and therapeutic tool. Healers, known as medicine men or women, use the wheel to understand the physical, emotional, mental, and spiritual aspects of a person's health. Each quadrant of the wheel is associated with specific elements, animals, and colors, which guide the healer in diagnosing and treating illnesses. This holistic approach to medicine reflects the belief that true healing requires addressing all aspects of a person's being.

The principles of the Medicine Wheel are also applied in Native American architecture, particularly in the design of communal spaces and ceremonial structures. Tipis, longhouses, and kivas are often arranged in circular patterns, reflecting the shape of the Medicine Wheel and the importance of unity and balance. These structures serve as centers for community gatherings, rituals, and teachings, reinforcing the connection between the physical space and the spiritual beliefs of the community.

The legacy of the Medicine Wheel continues to influence contemporary health and architectural practices. Modern healing centers and therapeutic spaces often incorporate elements of the Medicine Wheel, such as circular layouts and natural materials, to create environments that promote balance and well-being. This enduring symbol serves as a reminder of the profound wisdom of Native American cultures and their deep understanding of the interconnectedness of all life.

13

Chapter 11: The Renaissance Revival of Myth

The Renaissance period saw a revival of interest in classical mythology and its application in art, science, and architecture. Scholars and artists sought to rediscover and reinterpret the knowledge of the ancient Greeks and Romans, leading to innovations in medical practices and architectural design. This chapter examines the influence of mythological foundations on Renaissance medicine and architecture, highlighting the ways in which these ancient ideas were adapted and transformed during this pivotal era.

During the Renaissance, the rediscovery of classical texts by scholars such as Leonardo da Vinci and Andreas Vesalius sparked a renewed interest in the study of human anatomy and medicine. These scholars sought to reconcile the mythological teachings of ancient Greece and Rome with empirical observation and experimentation. Da Vinci's anatomical drawings, which combined artistic skill with scientific inquiry, reflect this synthesis of myth and reality. Vesalius's groundbreaking work, "De humani corporis fabrica," challenged traditional medical theories and laid the foundation for modern anatomy.

Renaissance architecture was also profoundly influenced by classical mythology. The works of architects such as Filippo Brunelleschi and Andrea

Palladio drew inspiration from the harmonious proportions and geometric principles of ancient Greek and Roman structures. The use of columns, arches, and domes in Renaissance buildings reflected the belief in a divine order that governed both the cosmos and human society. The incorporation of mythological motifs and symbols into the design of churches, palaces, and public buildings highlighted the enduring significance of these ancient stories in shaping the cultural and architectural landscape of the period.

The revival of classical mythology during the Renaissance extended to the visual arts as well. Painters such as Sandro Botticelli and Raphael used mythological themes and figures to explore complex human emotions and philosophical ideas. Botticelli's "The Birth of Venus," for example, draws on the myth of the goddess Venus to convey ideals of beauty, love, and divine inspiration. Raphael's frescoes in the Vatican's Stanza della Segnatura depict scenes from both classical mythology and Christian theology, reflecting the Renaissance belief in the interconnectedness of all knowledge.

The Renaissance revival of mythological foundations had a lasting impact on both medicine and architecture. The blending of classical knowledge with new scientific discoveries and artistic innovations laid the groundwork for future developments in these fields. The continued use of mythological symbols and motifs in contemporary medical and architectural practices serves as a testament to the enduring influence of these ancient stories on our understanding of the world.

14

Chapter 12: The Legacy of Myth in Modern Medicine and Architecture

Even in the modern world, the mythological foundations of medicine and architecture continue to resonate. From the symbolic use of the caduceus in medical logos to the incorporation of sacred geometry in contemporary building designs, these ancient beliefs have left an indelible mark on our cultural and scientific practices. In this final chapter, we reflect on the enduring legacy of myth in medicine and architecture, exploring how these timeless stories continue to inspire and inform our understanding of the world.

The caduceus, a staff entwined with two serpents, is a symbol deeply rooted in ancient mythology that continues to be used in modern medical practice. Although often confused with the Rod of Asclepius, the caduceus is associated with Hermes, the Greek messenger god. Its use as a symbol of medicine highlights the enduring influence of mythological imagery in contemporary healthcare. The caduceus serves as a reminder of the historical connection between mythology and medicine, symbolizing healing, transformation, and the pursuit of knowledge.

In architecture, the principles of sacred geometry continue to inspire modern designers and architects. The use of geometric patterns and proportions in contemporary buildings reflects the belief in a divine order that governs the universe. Structures such as the Guggenheim Museum in New York and the Sagrada Familia in Barcelona incorporate elements of sacred geometry, creating spaces that evoke a sense of harmony and balance. These designs draw on the ancient understanding of geometry as a reflection of the cosmos, demonstrating the lasting impact of mythological foundations on architectural innovation.

The legacy of mythological foundations in medicine is also evident in the holistic approach to healthcare that has gained prominence in recent years. Practices such as integrative medicine and functional medicine emphasize the interconnectedness of the body, mind, and spirit, reflecting ancient beliefs in the unity of all aspects of health. The incorporation of alternative therapies, such as acupuncture and herbal medicine, into mainstream healthcare highlights the continued relevance of mythological principles in modern medical practice.

As we look to the future, the enduring legacy of myth in medicine and architecture serves as a source of inspiration and a reminder of the timeless wisdom embedded in these ancient stories. By drawing on the rich tapestry of mythological beliefs and practices, we can continue to innovate and advance our understanding of the world, creating spaces and systems that promote health, harmony, and well-being. The myths of the past continue to shape our present and future, guiding us in our quest for knowledge and enlightenment.

15

Chapter 13: The Divine Proportion and the Human Body

The concept of the divine proportion, or the golden ratio, has fascinated mathematicians, artists, and architects for centuries. Rooted in ancient Greek philosophy, this mathematical ratio was believed to reflect the inherent harmony and beauty of the universe. The Greeks applied the golden ratio to their understanding of the human body, seeing it as a reflection of divine order. This chapter explores the mythological origins of the divine proportion and its application in medicine and architecture, demonstrating how this ancient concept continues to influence contemporary design and scientific thought.

In Greek mythology, the golden ratio was associated with the divine and the ideal. The philosopher Pythagoras and his followers believed that this ratio, represented by the Greek letter phi (φ), was a fundamental principle of the cosmos. They observed the golden ratio in nature, art, and architecture, and saw it as a reflection of the gods' perfect design. This belief in the mathematical harmony of the universe informed the Greeks' understanding of the human body and its proportions, which they saw as a microcosm of the divine order.

The influence of the golden ratio extended to the field of medicine, where it was used to study and analyze the human body. The ancient Greek physician

Hippocrates and later Renaissance anatomists such as Leonardo da Vinci and Andreas Vesalius applied the principles of the golden ratio to their anatomical studies. Da Vinci's famous drawing, the Vitruvian Man, illustrates the harmony and proportion of the human body based on the golden ratio. This integration of mathematics and anatomy reflects the enduring belief in the connection between the human body and the divine.

Architecturally, the golden ratio has been used to create harmonious and aesthetically pleasing designs. The Parthenon in Athens, the Great Pyramid of Giza, and the Cathedral of Notre-Dame are just a few examples of structures that incorporate the golden ratio in their design. These buildings reflect the belief in a divine order that governs both the cosmos and human creations. The continued use of the golden ratio in modern architecture and design demonstrates the timeless relevance of this ancient concept and its enduring impact on our understanding of beauty and harmony.

16

Chapter 14: The Symbolism of Light in Sacred Spaces

Light has always held a significant place in mythology and religion, symbolizing divine presence, knowledge, and enlightenment. Many ancient cultures used light as a central element in their architectural designs, creating spaces that reflected their spiritual beliefs and practices. This chapter explores the mythological significance of light and its application in the design of sacred spaces, from the temples of ancient Egypt to the cathedrals of medieval Europe, highlighting how light continues to inspire and influence contemporary architecture and healing environments.

In ancient Egypt, light was associated with the sun god Ra, who was believed to bring life and order to the world. The alignment of temples and monuments with the path of the sun was a common practice, reflecting the Egyptians' reverence for light and its divine symbolism. The Great Temple of Abu Simbel, for example, is designed so that twice a year, the rising sun illuminates the statues of the gods within the inner sanctuary, symbolizing their divine presence and power. This integration of light into architectural design underscores the Egyptians' belief in the connection between the physical and spiritual realms.

In medieval Europe, light played a central role in the design of cathedrals and churches. The use of stained glass windows, rose windows, and intricate tracery created a luminous and ethereal atmosphere that was intended to inspire awe and reverence. The Gothic cathedral, with its towering spires and expansive windows, sought to capture the divine light and bring it into the sacred space. The interplay of light and shadow within these buildings was seen as a reflection of the divine order and the presence of God, enhancing the spiritual experience of the worshippers.

The symbolism of light extends to modern architecture as well, where it is used to create spaces that promote healing, well-being, and spiritual connection. Hospitals, healing centers, and places of worship often incorporate natural light and open spaces to create environments that are conducive to health and tranquility. The use of light in contemporary design reflects the enduring belief in its transformative and uplifting power. This chapter highlights how the mythological significance of light continues to shape our understanding of space and its impact on the human experience.

17

Chapter 15: Mythological Inspirations in Contemporary Architecture

In the modern era, architects and designers continue to draw inspiration from mythological themes and symbols, creating innovative spaces that reflect ancient wisdom and contemporary aesthetics. This chapter explores the influence of mythology on contemporary architecture, showcasing examples of buildings and structures that incorporate mythological motifs, sacred geometry, and symbolic elements. From iconic skyscrapers to visionary eco-friendly designs, we examine how the enduring legacy of myth continues to inspire and shape the built environment.

One of the most striking examples of mythological inspiration in contemporary architecture is the Lotus Temple in New Delhi, India. Designed by architect Fariborz Sahba, this Bahá'í House of Worship takes the form of a lotus flower, a symbol of purity and spiritual enlightenment in Hindu and Buddhist mythology. The temple's unique design, with its 27 marble-clad petals arranged in three concentric circles, creates a serene and harmonious space for meditation and prayer. The Lotus Temple reflects the integration of mythological symbolism with modern engineering and aesthetics.

Another notable example is the Guggenheim Museum in Bilbao, Spain, designed by architect Frank Gehry. The museum's fluid and organic form, inspired by the shape of a fish, evokes the mythological association of water and transformation. Gehry's use of titanium, glass, and limestone creates a dynamic and reflective surface that interacts with the surrounding environment. The Guggenheim Museum represents the fusion of mythological themes with contemporary design, creating a space that is both visually stunning and symbolically rich.

Eco-friendly and sustainable architecture also draws inspiration from mythological and natural themes. The Eden Project in Cornwall, England, designed by architect Nicholas Grimshaw, is a visionary example of sustainable design inspired by the mythological concept of the Garden of Eden. The project features a series of geodesic domes that house diverse plant species from around the world, creating a biodiverse and self-sustaining environment. The Eden Project reflects the belief in the interconnectedness of all life and the importance of harmony with nature, drawing on ancient wisdom to address contemporary environmental challenges.

These examples demonstrate how contemporary architects and designers continue to be inspired by mythological themes, creating spaces that resonate with ancient wisdom while addressing modern needs and aesthetics. The enduring influence of mythology on architecture highlights the timeless relevance of these stories and their ability to inspire innovation and creativity. This chapter celebrates the rich tapestry of mythological inspiration in contemporary design, showcasing the power of myth to shape our understanding of the built environment and its impact on our lives.

Book Description:

"From Asgard to Anatomy: The Mythological Foundations of Medicine and Architecture" explores the rich tapestry of mythology and its profound influence on the development of medical practices and architectural designs throughout history. This captivating journey delves into the stories of gods, heroes, and ancient civilizations, revealing how their beliefs shaped the understanding of the human body and the built environment. From the healing sanctuaries of ancient Greece to the cosmic architecture of the Mayans, this book unveils the timeless wisdom embedded in mythological foundations and their enduring legacy in modern medicine and architecture.

www.ingramcontent.com/pod-product-compliance
Lightning Source LLC
LaVergne TN
LVHW020457080526
838202LV00057B/6014